「８」

この本には、８の無限の力が含まれています。

This book holds the infinite power of eight

富を生み出すために

To Generate Wealth

令和

Reiwa Period

By David.J.Nelson　デイビッド J. ネルソン著

この本を英語から日本語に翻訳したジョージ二宮氏と彼を紹介してくれたカタリーナ大里に感謝します。

Translated by Jorge Ninomiya
Contributions by Catarina Osato

五つ星レビュー

"素晴らしい８！" 東アジアの哲学に興味を持っている人、またはそれに携わっている人は誰でもこの本が気に入るはずです。 あなたは８を以前と同じ見方をすることは決してないだろう！」

Leslie Hutchison, Amazon review 2018 年 7 月 9 日

"特にアジアに住んでいる人のための魅力的な小さな本。"

読みやすい、面白い、役に立つ情報、オリジナル、気まぐれな、機知に富んだ内容。

Daniel F. Keller, BookBub、2018 年 7 月

これは必読の書です！ ネルソン氏は、８の力を理解し推進しています。これを読んでから、この数字に関連した幸運に恵まれて感謝しています。 ありがとうございました！"

J Jacob、Booksamillion、2018 年 9 月 4 日

5 Star Reviews

"Great 8! Anyone who has any interest in, or connection to, East Asian philosophy will love this book. You'll never look at an 8 the same!"

Leslie Hutchison, Amazon review July 9, 2018

"Charming little book, especially for anyone who has lived in Asia. Easy-to-read; Entertaining; Informative; Original; Whimsical; Witty

Daniel F. Keller, BookBub, July 2018

"This book is a must read! Mr. Nelson understands and promotes the power of 8. Since reading this, I appreciate the good fortune associated with this number. Thank You!"

J Jacob, Booksamillion, September 4, 2018

"全ての物に美しさはあるが、全ての人にそれが見えている
訳ではない" 孔子

"Everything has beauty, but not everyone sees it."

Confucius

この著書を息子アンドレに捧げる

I dedicate this book to my son Andre.

読者の方へ

私がアジアに住んでいる間に 8 と交流している人々を見たときに私がどのように感じたかを説明するのに最も適切な言葉は、魅惑です。 8 はその地域で強力な象徴的および金銭的価値を持っているので、発見の旅に私を導きました。 私はこの世界のいたるところで 8 の数字を見つけ始めました。 私が研究し、探求するほど、私はこの驚異的な数についてより多くの事実を発見しました。 実は 8 の力の裏にはかなりの歴史があります。 文化を超えて、宗教文学や科学的観察において 8 の数字が際立って現れるのは驚くべきことです。 地球上の 8 の力の遍在は単なる偶然の一致でしょうか？ 私はそうは思いません。 8 の力は、世界中のあらゆるところを包み込みます。 今、私と共にこの旅に参加して下さってありがとう。あなたも私と一緒に 8 の世界に入り、ゆったりと腰を落ち着けて、深呼吸をして、そして 8 の乗り心地を楽しんでください！

TO THE READER

Fascinated is the best word to describe how I felt when I watched people interacting with the number eight during my years living in Asia. Eight has such powerful symbolic and monetary value in that region that it sent me on a journey of discovery. I started to find the number eight everywhere in this world. The more I researched and explored, the more facts I found about this phenomenal number. There is actually substantial history behind eight's power. Ranging across cultures, it is amazing how often the number eight appears prominently in religious literature and in scientific observation. Is the omnipresence of eight's power on the planet just a coincidence? I don't think so. The power of eight envelopes the world everywhere. For now, I want to thank you for joining me on this journey. Now that you have already entered the world of eight with me, just settle back, get comfortable, take a deep breath, and enjoy eight's ride!

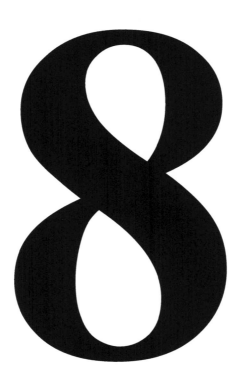

I.   なぜあなたは数字 8 を気にする必要があるのでしょうか？

1. アジアでは、8 が明白な力を発揮します。

2. 8 はアジアの不動産で真価を発揮します。

3. 人々は中国で数字 8 に対して、より多くの金額を支払います。

4. 香港で売られた 8 の数字が付いているナンバープレートの価格：＄230万。

5. 8 階のアパートは、高額で売れる。

6. 中国での大成功：2008年8月8日に開催された北京オリンピック。

7. 中国だけでなく、アジア全体で数字 8 の価値は認められています。

8. 8 の文章を読まれました。あなたはラッキーです。

I. Why should you care about the number eight?

1. In Asia, the number eight projects palpable power.

2. Eight holds real value in Asian real estate.

3. People pay more in China for number eight.

4. Number eight Hong Kong license plate sold: $2,300,000.

5. Apartments on the eighth floor are more valuable.

6. Big Chinese success: Beijing Olympics, August eighth, 2008.

7. Not only China, but all Asia values eight.

8. You read eight sentences: now luck you have.

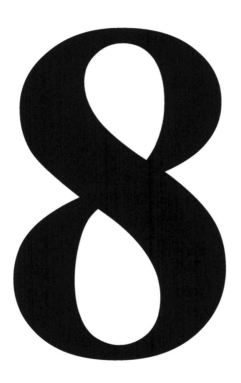

II. これが 8 に関するいくつかの事実です。

1. 中国で 8 は、「金持ちになる」という意味があります。

2. 酸素の原子番号は 8 です。

3. 1バイトのコンピュータデータは 8 ビットです。

4. 私たちの太陽系は、まだ 8つの惑星で生き残っています。

5. 科学によると、「オクトニアン」は弦理論の中で力を有しています。

6. キリスト教徒、仏教徒、ヒンズー教徒、ユダヤ教徒、そしてイスラム教徒は 8 を尊重します。

7. ユダヤ人はハヌカー(ヘブライ語で捧げる)を合計 8日間祝います。

8. 8 は無限の記号を縦にしたものです。

II. Here are some facts about the number eight.

1. Eight in Chinese sounds like "to become rich."

2. The atomic number designation for Oxygen is 8.

3. One byte of computer data is 8 bits.

4. Our solar system still survives with 8 planets.

5. Science says "octonians" have power within string theory.

6. Christians, Buddhists, Hindus, Jewish, and Muslims respect eight.

7. The Jewish celebrate Chanukah for eight days total.

8. Eight is the vertical upright symbol of infinity.

III. 聖書には、数字 8 が多く使われています。

1. 聖書の中で 8 は73回使われています。

2. イエス・キリストは 8日目に復活しました。

3. 幕屋の饗宴は 8 日間続きました。

4. 神とアブラハムとの契約は全て8つでした。

5. 旧約聖書には8曲あります。

6. 888という数字は神の象徴です。

7. ノアの箱舟は合計8人を救いました。

8. エリヤの奇跡の総数は8でした。

III. The bible is filled with the number eight:

1. Eight is used 73 times in the bible.

2. Jesus Christ was resurrected on the eighth day.

3. The Feast of Tabernacles lasted for eight days.

4. All the Lord's covenants with Abraham totaled eight.

5. There are eight songs in the Old Testament.

6. The number 888 is the symbol of God.

7. Noah's Ark saved a total of eight people.

8. The total number of Elijah's miracles was eight.

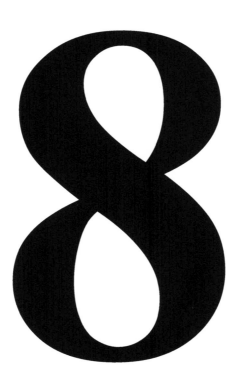

IV.　数字の8は仏教の中で最高のものです。

1. ニルヴァーナ（悟り）　に導くのは 聖なる８つの正しい道です。

2. 理解、見解、思考、言論、努力、行動、注意深さ、集中力。

3. 仏教宣教師は、8つの縁起の良い象徴を中国にもたらしました。

4. 円形の「Dharmacakra」仏教シンボルには8本のスポークがあります。

5. 仏様は8つの「ジャナ」とも呼ばれる8つの達成を強調しました。

6. 仏教によると8つのすばらしい菩薩が存在します。

7. 8は中国の「不滅」の正確な数です。

8. 12月8日は、日本におけるお釈迦様の誕生日のお祝いです。

IV. The number eight is also paramount in Buddhism:

1. To achieve Nirvana (enlightenment), the path is eightfold.

2. Understanding, view, thought, speech, effort, action, mindfulness, concentration.

3. Buddhist missionaries brought eight auspicious symbols to China.

4. The circular "Dharmacakra" Buddhist symbol has eight spokes.

5. Buddha emphasized eight attainments also called eight "jhanas."

6. There are eight great Bodhisattvas according to Buddhism.

7. Eight is the exact number of Chinese "Immortals."

8. Celebration of Buddha's Birthday: eighth of the month.

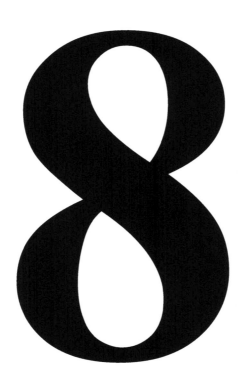

V. 8 についての詩を思い出して暗唱して下さい。

1. この詩は強力な数字 8 についてです。

2. 各8文の韻律に注目してください。

3. 8 が私と共にいる限り、全てがうまく行きます。

4. 8つのエネルギーが水のように流れ、私を強く
   します。

5. 　何処へ行こうとも、数字8とこの著書のこと
   は忘れません。

6. 私の8人の敵は逃げて、私の8人の同盟者は成長します。

7. 8 はどの単独な敵よりも強力です。

8. 私が植え付けた8つの考えから富を得て下さい。

V. Remember and recite a poem about number eight:

1. This poem is about the powerful number eight.

2. Notice the cadence with each sentence of eight.

3. When eight is with me, nothing goes wrong.

4. Eight's energy flows like water, making me strong.

5. Forget what I will, but this I know.

6. My eight enemies flee, my eight allies grow.

7. Eight is more powerful than any single foe.

8. Reap wealth from thoughts of eight I sew.

EIGHT

「8」

内含8的無限力量
The Spiritual Healing Power of Eight

David J. Nelson

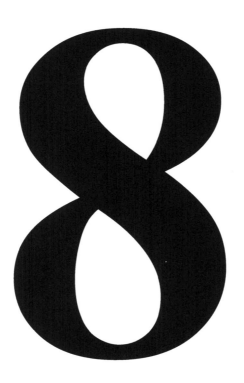

VI.　科学的証拠は 8 の力を示していますか？

1. 科学は8の力の事例で満たされています。

2. 8個の核子が原子核内に完全な殻を作ります。

3. 8 =フィボナッチ数列の最大の３乗数字。

4. オクテットにはちょうど8ビットあります。

5. 人間の血液型の数は8です。

6. 1つの殻にいくつ電子が存在するか：8。

7. キューブを形成するには8つの頂点が必要です。

8. 光は太陽から地球へ到達するには８分かかります。

VI. Does scientific evidence point to number eight's power?

1. Science is filled with examples of eight's power.

2. Eight nucleons make complete shells within atomic nucleus.

3. Eight = largest cube number in the Fibonacci sequence.

4. There are exactly eight bits in an Octet.

5. Number of blood types for humans is eight.

6. How many electrons reside in a shell: eight.

7. Eight vertices are needed to form a cube.

8. Light travels from sun to earth: eight minutes.

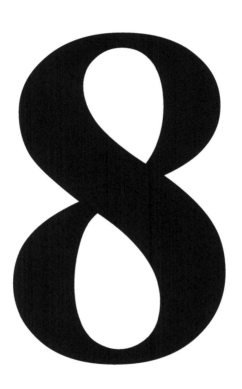

VII. 8の力をどのように利用しますか。

1. あなたがしていること全ての中で8を探し出して
    下さい。

2. あなたの成功を援助する8つのことを想像して下さい。

3. あなたが所有している全てに番号8を付けます。

4. ポケットには常に8つのものを入れて下さい。

5. 8ドル、8円、または8ペソを保ちます。

6. あなたが愛する家族の8つの宝物。

7. この本は常にあなたと一緒に維持してください。

8.   この本を8人の親友と共有しましょう。

VII. How do you harness the power of eight?

1. You seek out eight in all you do.

2. Imagine eight things that will help you succeed.

3. Attach number eight to all that you own.

4. Always keep eight of something in your pocket.

5. Keep eight dollars, eight Yuan, or eight pesos.

6. Treasure eight of your family who you love.

7. Keep this book with you at all times.

8. Share this book with your eight best friends.

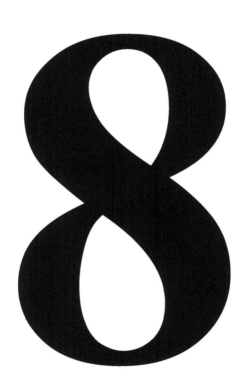

VIII. 何故 8 が富のひとつなのでしょうか。

1. 古いスペインの硬貨は「8の部分」と呼ばれて
   いました。

2. 米国連邦準備貨幣のシリアルナンバーは8桁です。

3. 数字 8 はあなたに富を創造します。

4. 2018年8月8日、アジアにおける活発な活動を観察
   して下さい。

5. 次の年において、今すぐビジネスを計画して
   下さい。

6. 2028, 2038, 2048, 2058, 2068, 2078, 2088.

7. 今すぐあなたの心の中で数字8を想像してみて
   下さい。

8. この本を持って、8の力を有して下さい。

VIII. How the number eight is one with wealth:

1. Old Spanish coins were called "pieces of eight."

2. U.S. Federal reserve note serials have eight digits.

3. The number eight can create wealth for you.

4. Observe significant activity in Asia, August eighth 2018.

5. Plan your business now for the following dates:

6. August 2028, 2038, 2048, 2058, 2068, 2078, 2088.

7. Imagine the number eight in your mind now.

8. Hold this book: hold the power of 8.

「8」

內含8的無限力量
This book holds the infinite power of eight

8

To Generate Wealth
齊來致富

By David.J.Nelson

Amazon Hot New Releases

EIGHT

8

This Book Holds the Infinite Power of Eight

David Nelson

謝辞

私の息子と妻のレッティーは、何かを創造することを考えてから実際にそれを実行することへの飛躍において、私をやる気にさせてくれました。私がニューヨークのグッゲンハイムでアート作品を批評していた時に私を見て、実際にその芸術家の作品がそれほど高額な価格をする印象はないかも知れないと言いました。しかし、「この芸術家とあなたの違いは、彼はそこから出て、何かを生み出したことだ」と言いました。レッティーは私の目を見て、こう言いました。「もし、あなたがこれ以上のものを創れると思うなら、それを実行に移すべきです。」

私の親愛なる友人エリックA. は私にこの仕事を、ちょうど8つの章に構成するというアイデアを授けてくれました。その独創的なアイデアのおかげで、今日では8つの章だけでなく各章に8つの文があり、すべての文に英語で正確に8つの単語が含まれています。

フィリピンで働くことによって、私は非常に多くの素晴らしい人々に出会うことが出来ました。このプロジェクトを続けるよう私を励ましてくれた同僚の一人はポールSでした。ポールは天才で非常に批判的な思想家です。彼がこの本の前提を拒否しなかった時、私は自分が何かやりがいのあることに出会っていたことに気づきました。ポール、私のアイデアを笑わないでくれてありがとう！

それから私の人生の全て、又は大部分に愛と支持を与えてくれた人々がいます。ナンシーとジムはもちろんそのリストの一番上にいます。彼らは、私をこの世界に導き、そして私が生き残るために必要なものを与えてくれました。

それから私の姉妹メグとダニエレがいます。彼女らは私が心から愛している世界で最も強くて最も美しい女性のうちの2人です。彼女らの父ラス（故人）は、私が常により良くなるように私に挑戦していたので、私の人生にも非常に影響力がありました。

コネチカット州に住むグアンダリーニ家族全員が、私を今日の自分にしてくれたのです。　　Jean、Joe、Judy、Henry、Marian、Dave、Tommy、Pete G、Cindy、Pete H、そしてその家族全員が私のヒーローであり、私のインスピレーションです。

レッティーの母親ロザリーナは、私の人生の愛する妻をこの世に導きました。

多くの素晴らしい人々がこの人生の旅を通して私を取り囲んで来ました。あなた方の名前が全てここにリストされていないかもしれませんが、あなたは誰であるかを知っているとともに私があなたを愛し感謝していることをご存じです。

Acknowledgements

My son and my wife Letty got me motivated to make the leap from thinking about creating something to actually doing it. Checking me when I was critiquing some art work at the Guggenheim in New York, they told me that it may be true that the artist's work was, perhaps, not that impressive to hold such exorbitant monetary value. However, they said "the difference between this artist and you is that the artist got out there and produced something." Letty looked me in the eyes and said "if you think you could make something better, then you should go and do it."

My dear friend Eric A. gave me the idea to structure this work into exactly eight chapters. That ingenious idea brought me to where we ended up today with not only eight chapters but also eight sentences in each chapter- and every sentence contains exactly eight words.

Working in the Philippines introduced me to so many amazing people. One of my colleagues who encouraged me to continue with this project was Paul S. Paul is a genius and a very critical thinker. When he did not shoot the premise of the book down, I knew I was onto something. Thank you for not laughing Paul!

Then there are all the people who have given me love and support for all or most of my life. Nancy and Jim of course are at the very top of that list. They brought me into this world and then gave me what I needed to survive and to thrive.

Then come my sisters Meg and Danielle. They are two of the strongest and most beautiful women in the world who I love with all my heart. Their father Russ (in memory) was also very influential in my life as he always challenged me to be better.

All of my extended Guandalini family in Connecticut made me into who I am today. Jean, Joe, Judy, Henry, Marian, Dave, Tommy, Pete G, Cindy, Pete H, and all of their families are my heroes and my inspiration.

Letty's mother Rosalina brought the love of my life into this world.

A special thanks to Jorge Ninomiya who is such a skilled, patient, and dedicated Master of translation! A very special thanks to my dear friend and colleague, Catarina Osato. Thank you so much Cata and I could not have done this without you!

So many wonderful people have surrounded me through this journey of life. All of your names may not be listed here but you know who you are and you know that I love and appreciate you.

著者について

David J. Nelsonは、ジョージア大学で政治学において文学士号を取得しました。 オタワ大学で国際政治学および比較政治学の修士号も取得しています。彼は妻のレティ、息子のアンドレ、そして犬の「ジュリー」と暮らしています。彼らの家の番地は8です。

Check David's web site often for fun facts about 8, latest news and publications!
https://infinite88888888.com/

Follow David at:
https://www.facebook.com/Eight-8-2154878644542235/
https://instagram.com/8888davidjnelson8888?utm_source=ig_profile_share&igshid=3em38c158430

About the author

David J. Nelson earned his B.A. in Political Science from the University of Georgia and he also holds a M.A. in International and Comparative Politics from the University of Ottawa. He lives with his wife Letty, his son Andre, and his dog "Julie." The street address of their home is 8.

Follow David in the social media:

FaceBook: https://www.facebook.com/Eight-8-2154878644542235/

https://instagram.com/8888davidjnelson8888?utm_source=ig_profile_share&igshid=3em38c158430

Check his web site often for fun facts about 8 latest news and publications!

https://infinite88888888.com/

参考文献: References:

- https://sites.google.com/site/numberopedia/number8inscienceandtech

- https://en.wikipedia.org/wiki/8

- http://www.newworldencyclopedia.org/entry/8_(number)

- https://www.nytimes.com/2016/02/23/world/asia/hong-kong-car-license-plate.html

- http://www.astrovera.com/bible-religion/189-bible-number-8.html

- https://tricycle.org/magazine/noble-eightfold-path/

- https://mysticalnumbers.com/number-8-in-buddhism/

- https://www.numerology.com/numerology-numbers/8

Back Cover

I am honored to present the edition of this book in both Japanese and English. Designed for all readers from 8 to 888 years old. It brings world culture, languages, and intriguing facts about the number 8.

Why do billions of people believe that the number 8 symbolizes prosperity and good fortune? Eight has tangible power and value in Asia. Eight in Chinese sounds like "to generate wealth." Did you know that the Chinese chose the following date to bring luck and success to the Beijing Olympic Games: 08/08/2008?

Unlock the power of eight and harness the symbolism to your advantage in business, and in life. Begin to see the science and history that explain how to leverage the number as a symbol of prosperity. You can read this book anytime for inspiration and good luck. This book inspires the reader to achieve wealth, love, health, and happiness. This bilingual version of the book is a wonderful educational tool for both English and Japanese language learners. It contains original, beautiful, and artistic photography for a fun read that is easy on the eyes. The book in Japanese maintains the same format of the book in English: There are 8 chapters. Each chapter has 8 sentences.

Special thanks to Jorge Ninomiya, who translated this book from English to Japanese, and to Catarina Osato, who introduced him to the author.

About the Author

David's favorite hobbies include reading, hiking, writing, learning about different cultures and how they connect to each other. His passion for learning about new cultures started when David lived in Japan as a child in the 1980's. Living in Haiti, Zambia, Switzerland, Morocco, France, Canada, Brazil, Mexico, and the Philippines transformed his international experience into a passion for the Arts. It shaped his studies and career as a diplomat. David J. Nelson earned his B.A. in Political Science from the University of Georgia and he also holds a M.A. from the University of Ottawa.

免責事項

作者と出版社はこの本の情報が印刷時に正しいことを保証するためにあらゆる努力を払っていますが、作者と出版社は誤り、または損失によって引き起こされたいかなる損失、損害または混乱についてもいかなる責任も負いません。 それが怠慢、誤り、または脱落が、過失、事故、またはその他の原因のいずれかに起因しても責任は負いません。

この著書はあなたの娯楽と楽しみのためのものです。

Disclaimer

Although the author and publisher have made every effort to ensure that the information in this book was correct at press time, the author and publisher do not assume and hereby disclaim any liability to any party for any loss, damage, or disruption caused by errors or omissions, whether such errors or omissions result from negligence, accident, or any other cause.

This book is for your entertainment and enjoyment.

41873503R00033

Made in the USA
Middletown, DE
10 April 2019